The
Viking
Library

Viking
Families and Farms

Andrea Hopkins, Ph.D.

The Rosen Publishing Group's
PowerKids Press™
New York

To my mother and father
Descended from those that made the Danelaw

Published in 2002 by The Rosen Publishing Group, Inc.
29 East 21st Street, New York, NY 10010

First Edition

Book Design and Layout: Michael Caroleo

Project Editor: Frances E. Ruffin

Photo Credits: Title page (pottery and skate), pp. 3 (all), 4 (spoons and pottery), 8 (fish hooks), 15 (combs, knife with sheath), 16 (table set) © York Archaeological Trust; title page and p. 7 (longhouse) © William W. Fitzhugh, NMNH; p. 4 (buckle end) © Werner Forman Archive/Universitetets Oldsaksamling, Oslo, (Faroe Islands) © Símun V. Arge; p. 7 (longhouse diagram) research provided by Faeroese Historical Museum, Tórshavn; p. 8 (Borg, Loften, Norway) © Karsten Kristiansen Courtesy Tromsø University Museum; p. 8 (scythes) © Peter Harholdt, NMNH; p. 11 (watercolor on paper by W.G. Collingwood 1897) Courtesy Trustees of The British Museum, London; p. 12 © Walter Bibikow/The Viesti Collection Inc.; p. 15 (wood panel) © The Art Archive/Oldsaksammlung Oslo/Dagli Orti; p. 15 (sword) © Matti Huuhka, Museokuva, National Board of Antiquities; p. 15 (spear) © Hulkkunanmaki, Lieto, Finland, National Board of Antiquities; p. 16 (tapestry) © Werner Forman Archive/Viking Ship Museum, Bygdoy; p. 16 (costume reinactment) © Ulla Finnila, Kalevla Koru Limited Center for Handicraft, Heinola; p. 19 © North Wind Pictures; p. 20 (Birka) © Jan Normann, RAA/Courtesy of Museum of National Antiquities, Stockholm; p. 20 (map) © Map Art.

Images on title page and pp. 7(longhouse), 4(Faroe Islands), 8(Borg and scythes), 11, 15(sword and spear), 16(female costume), 20(Birka) courtesy of the Artic Studies Center, Smithsonian National Museum of Natural History.

Hopkins, Andrea.
Viking Families and Farms / Andrea Hopkins.— 1st ed.
    p. cm. — (The Viking library)
Includes index.
ISBN 0-8239-5815-9
1. Northmen—Social life and customs—Juvenile literature. 2. Vikings—Social life and customs—Juvenile literature. 3. Farm life—Scandinavia—History—Juvenile literature. 4. Scandinavia—Social life and customs—Juvenile literature. I. Title. II. Series.
DL65 .H68 2002
948'.022—dc21

00-012310

Contents

The Vikings at Home

Beginning in A.D. 793, and for 300 years after that, Norsemen who were known as Vikings left their homes to **raid**, **loot**, and kill all over Europe. Not all Norse people went "viking," though. Most people who lived in Norway, Sweden, and Denmark were farmers. A Viking farm could be small, with just enough land to support one family. It could be a large farm where a wealthy family, their **slaves**, and the freemen who worked for them all lived together.

This reconstruction of a Norse farm is on the Faroe Islands, which lie in the North Atlantic. Some items dug up on what had been Norse farms include (from the top left) the end of a belt, wooden spoons, and a large bowl.

Every Norse farm had a longhouse, smaller buildings, fields for crops, and pastures for the animals. Viking farmers produced most of their own food, clothes, tools, and furniture. They also fished, hunted, and trapped wild animals for meat and fur.

The Longhouse

At the center of every farm was the longhouse. This was the main building where everyone lived, worked, ate, and slept. It had a long hall that was divided into a big room in the middle and two smaller ones at each end. Food was prepared in one small room. The other was a barn for cattle. An open pit at the center of the hall had a fire for cooking. Smoke escaped through a hole in the roof. There were no windows. There were no bedrooms. Only the head of the family had a bed closet for privacy. Everyone else slept on sleeping platforms. There were no beds, tables, or chairs. Bedding, clothes, and tools were stored in chests, which also were used as seats. People ate meals on long boards set on wooden supports. The longhouse was lit by the cooking fire and small oil lamps.

This reconstructed longhouse is in Iceland. The two drawings show the layout of a longhouse, which included animal stalls, space for storage, and a large hall.

STORAGE
Loose

POST
HOLE
Skelpaheal

LONG HEARTH

DRAIN
Drain

Longrid

Hellen

HALL

Stone

ANIMAL
STALLS

Viking Farming

Farms varied from country to country. The land was mountainous in Norway and northern Sweden. Few crops could be grown there. Instead, farmers raised cattle and sheep and used natural **resources** such as timber and iron. Farms there and in Iceland were **isolated** from their neighbors. In Denmark and southern Sweden, the land was flatter and many crops were grown, including rye and wheat for bread, oats, cabbages, peas, onions, beans, and barley. These farms were in villages and were grouped together. All Norse farmers kept animals.

The photo shows what had been the large farm of a Viking chieftain who lived in a far northern area of Norway. Tools used for plowing crops (far left) and fish hooks (right) have been dug up on the sites of Viking farms.

Norsemen who lived near water fished. They dried fish for eating during the winter. Viking farmers who wanted goods they couldn't make or hunt produced a surplus of their own goods and traded them. In this way, most farms managed to get imported goods like glass, spices, silk, and precious metals, like gold.

The Viking Family

Family life was the most important part of the Viking world. A person had a first name, such as Olaf or Astrid, but second names almost always referred to being someone's son or daughter. For example, a person would be named Olaf Karlsson, or Astrid Karlsdaughter. In Iceland today, men are still called their father's sons, and women their mother's daughters. Anyone who was related to you was part of your **kin**. If someone in your family was hurt by others, it was your duty to **avenge** them, often by killing the others. Sometimes the killings would go on until almost every member of a family was wiped out.

Iceland had a national assembly every three years, called Althing. This painting shows the meeting at a rock formation called Thingvellir.

Viking people agreed that laws could settle disagreements. Several families would get together at public meetings. These meetings took place regularly. They were called Things. Crimes such as thefts, killings, and arguments over land ownership were discussed and settled at the Things.

Slaves

Slaves were often people who had been captured in Viking raids on foreign countries. Many were bought and sold at slave markets. Some slaves were Norse people who had lost their freedom as punishment for a crime. Occasionally very poor people sold themselves into slavery if they couldn't support themselves. Slaves who were strong and had skills were valuable. Some slaves had special skills in metalworking or wood carving. At times, these slaves were allowed to earn extra money to buy their freedom. They wore metal collars. Slaves did the hardest and the least important tasks. They cleaned the house, fed and cleaned animals, gathered firewood, and did other chores. Their owners could beat and even kill the slaves if they did not obey.

◀ *This exhibit shows a Norse workman. Slaves and freemen were valued for their skills in metalworking and carpentry.*

Men's Work

Norsemen hunted, fished, and looked after farm animals. They made their own tools and mended fishing nets and sails. Every man had to be a skilled carpenter. Men built houses and boats and made wagons, sleds, and other objects from wood. Some men became good "smiths," people who worked with metal. They were important members of the Viking community. Smiths made metal tools and weapons from iron ore. Most farms had a smithy. Tools also were made from wood, stone, bones, and ivory from walrus tusks.

The background image is a wood carving on the door of Hylestad Church in Setesdal, Norway. Other examples of Norse workmanship include combs made of bone (top left), *a sword and spear* (bottom left), *and an iron knife and leather sheath* (right).

Carving was a favorite way of passing the time. Men carved useful things like combs or handles from ivory or reindeer antlers. They put decorations on all kinds of everyday objects. They also made amazing carvings on large objects such as doors, benches, and ships' prows, which were the pointed fronts of ships.

14

This woman is dressed in a style of clothing that was typical of clothes worn by Norse women.
The images at the far left show examples of Norse cups, bowls, and spoons. The textile sample came from an excavation. The extremely cold soil in Northern Europe helped to preserve Norse textiles.

Women's Work

Norse women's work, besides cleaning and cooking, included spinning and weaving wool cloth. They made all kinds of **textiles** for clothing. They made butter and cheese and brewed ale for drinking. They **preserved** food to keep it from spoiling. Although they did not have the same rights as men, they enjoyed a great deal more freedom than women in other European countries. They could own property, trade goods, and divorce their husbands if they wanted to. Norse women were proud of their skills and were valued for them. Women often acted as heads of households when their husbands went on Viking **expeditions**. The wife of a Viking had to run the house and the farm. She directed the slaves and freemen in their work. She was a valuable partner in the family Viking business.

Colonizing

Viking men had a poor opinion of farming as a way of life. That was something for women and slaves, or for men too old to go to sea. Young, strong men knew that it was much more **profitable** to go viking. They could become rich and could gain great respect. For many Vikings, stories of what they or their **ancestors** had done on Viking raids were almost more important than the loot they had stolen. They believed that it was better to be killed while fighting in some foreign raid than to die on your back in straw, like a cow. Even the great Viking adventurers wanted to **colonize**, to take over new lands and to start their own **communities**, which were almost always big farms. The great **ambition** of Norse people was to own a big, **prosperous** farm. Land was the measure of a man's wealth and success.

Although Vikings believed that it was noble to be killed while fighting in a raid, the great ambition for most Norsemen was to own a big, prosperous farm. ▶

18

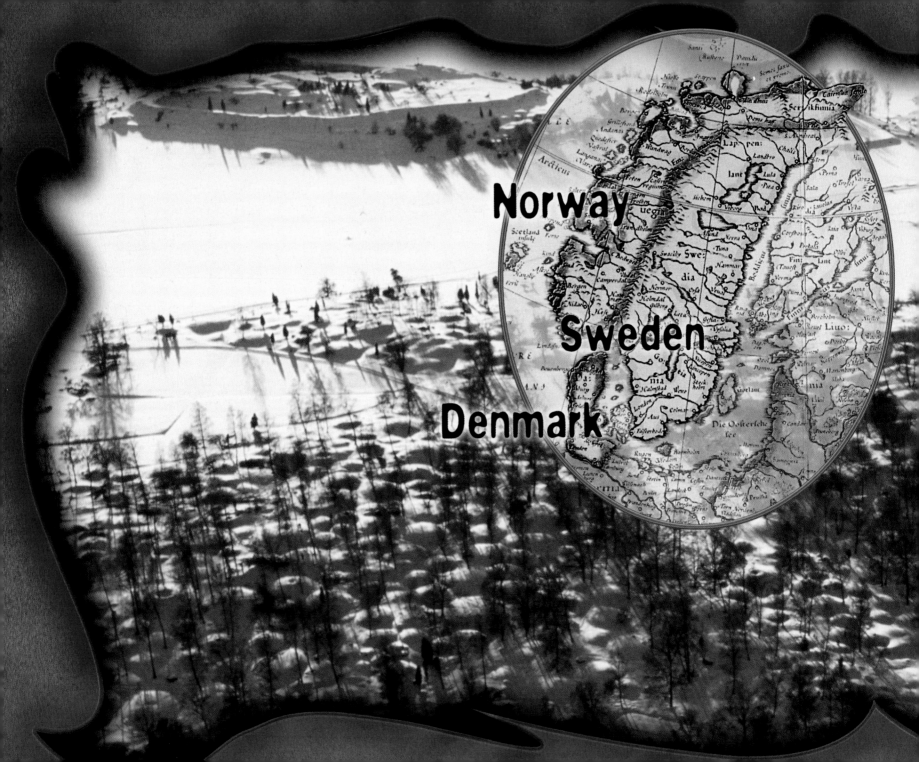

Norway

Sweden

Denmark

Winter on the Farm

Viking expeditions always took place in the summer. The men who had gone viking would come back to **Scandinavia** during the winter. Their longships would be laid up and the Vikings would go home to their wives and families. Winters were hard in Scandinavian countries. The days were short and the weather was bitterly cold. Farm animals, such as cattle and pigs, had to be brought indoors for the winter. Sheep usually were left outside to fend for themselves. On many farms, the cattle and pigs lived through the winter in a room inside the longhouse. The cattle ate hay and the pigs ate leftover food and garbage. You can just imagine the noise and the smell in a longhouse! Winter was also a time when Norse people visited each other and held parties and feasts.

◄ *This map of Scandinavia has a background photograph of a winter scene at Birka, Sweden. Birka was a large trading center for the Norse during the 700s and 800s.*

Viking Feasts

Norse people loved to open their homes to guests. They offered their visitors the best food and drink, and the most comfortable places to sleep. Giving feasts and parties was a good way to show off wealth. The most important event of the winter season was the great Yule feast, which took place on December 25. Feasts usually lasted for several days, so you had to be quite wealthy to give one. Meat was roasted over a fire or was boiled in a huge pot with broth. White bread was served at feasts, not the brown, lumpy, everyday bread. Viking feasts were also occasions for entertainment. There was singing. There were games and shows of strength. If the party givers were very lucky, there might be a fight.

Glossary

ambition (am-BIH-shun) The desire to do well.

ancestors (AN-ses-turz) Relatives who lived long ago.

avenge (uh-VENJ) To get even for a wrongdoing.

colonize (KAH-luh-nyz) To settle in a new land.

communities (kuh-MYOO-nih-teez) Groups of people or animals that live in the same place.

expeditions (ek-spuh-DIH-shunz) Trips for a special purpose.

isolated (EYE-suh-layt-ed) Placed apart and alone.

kin (KIN) Family and other blood relatives.

loot (LOOT) To take another person's property by force.

preserved (pruh-ZURVD) Prepared food in a way that kept it from spoiling.

profitable (PRAH-fih-tuh-buhl) Giving wealth or profit.

prosperous (PRAHS-peh-rus) Wealthy, successful.

raid (RAYD) A surprise attack by a group of well-armed people.

resources (REE-sors-es) A supply or source of energy or useful materials.

Scandinavia (scan-dih-NAY-vee-ah) Northern Europe, usually Norway, Sweden, and Denmark.

slaves (SLAYVZ) People who are "owned" by other people and are forced to work for them.

textiles (TEK-stylz) Woven fabric or cloth.

Index

C
colonize, 18

D
Denmark, 5, 9

E
expeditions, 17, 21

F
feasts, 21, 22
freemen, 5, 17

I
Iceland, 9, 10
iron, 9, 14

L
longhouse, 6, 21

M
metalworking, 13

N
Norway, 5, 9

R
raid(s), 5, 13, 18
resources, 9

S
Scandinavia, 21
slaves, 5, 13, 17, 18
stories, 18
Sweden, 5, 9

T
textiles, 17

W
winter, 21
women's rights in Viking
    families, 17
wood carving, 13

Web Sites

To learn more about Viking families and farms, check out these Web sites:
http://viking.no/e/life/ewomen.htm
www.regia.org/earner.htm

24